UNEARTHING ANCIENT CIVILIZATIONS



# ANCIENT GREECE REVEALED

BY DONNA REYNOLDS

Cavendish Square
New York

The Aegean Sea played a large part in the growth of ancient Greece. In some places, bridges such as this one needed to be built.

# CHAPTER ONE

# THE FIRST EUROPEAN CIVILIZATION

Civilization in Europe began much later than it did in Africa, Asia, and the Middle East. Around 3000 BCE, the first European civilization rose near the Aegean Sea in what is today the country of Greece. They were called the Minoans, which comes from their leader, Minos. Today, **experts** are not sure whether Minos was the name of one ruler or a title that was used by every ruler.

## THE MINOANS

The Minoans lived on the island of Crete. They were seafaring traders with a powerful navy. Living on an island can **isolate** a civilization, but the opposite was true for the Minoans. They were well known for trading. Their island did not have many natural **resources**, so they traded to get things they needed to build their civilization. One of the most important was bronze, which is a metal made up of copper and tin. With bronze, people could make tools, weapons, jewelry, and many other things. It was such an important item that the period of time when its use became popular is called the Bronze Age.

Shown here are the remains of a Minoan palace in Knossos, which was the center of the Minoan civilization.

The Minoans were some of the first in Europe to learn how to make bronze, but because they did not have copper and tin on their island, they needed to build boats and take to the sea. The people they came into contact with, such as the Egyptians, kept records of what was traded. From these records, historians can tell that the Minoans mostly made and traded things people wanted rather than needed. These included metal artwork, fancy pottery, and makeup. Trade helped make the Minoans wealthy, so they were able to **expand** around 1580 BCE. Some of them moved onto mainland Greece, taking their **culture** with them. However, Crete was still the center of Minoan life.

### THE SECRET OF PURPLE

Many people wanted to trade with the Minoans for one thing only they could make: purple dye. A sea snail called a murex lived around the island, and the Minoans figured out how to use it to make purple dye. It takes thousands of these sea snails to make even a little bit of dye, so it was very expensive and highly valued. This is why purple came to be known as the color of royalty.

## THE RISE OF THE MYCENAEANS

Around 1600 BCE, a huge volcanic eruption happened on the island of Thera, which is now called Santorini. Thera was only about 70 miles (112 kilometers) from Crete, and experts are sure it affected the Minoans. It did not kill them, but it did make life harder. One of the biggest effects of a volcanic eruption is clouds of ash that harm crops and block out the sun. Experts believe it is likely that this caused a famine, or period of little to no food, on Crete that helped bring about the fall of Minoan society.

Like the Minoans, the Mycenaeans made beautiful works of art. This fresco, or wall painting, was found in the ruins at Mycenae.

After the fall of the Minoans, the Mycenaeans took power. Their name comes from their main city, Mycenae, which was located on the Greek mainland. Like the Minoans, they started trading with other groups. Because the Minoans had started moving into other parts of Greece, the Mycenaeans were also **influenced** by their culture. However, they changed parts of it to make it their own. Their culture influenced later Greek cultures, and their myths about people and events, such as Achilles, Odysseus, and the Trojan War, are still well known today.

Linear B (*shown here*) was the Mycenaean alphabet. It looks nothing like the modern-day Greek alphabet.

# CHAPTER TWO
## THE DARK AGE

There are fewer records for ancient Greek society than there are for many other ancient civilizations, so not much is known about how the Mycenaean civilization fell. However, we do know it happened around 1200 BCE. From then until about 800 BCE, Greece entered a time some historians call the Dark Age. This is because the population decreased and the Greek civilization broke into many small, separate cities.

### A BACKWARD TIME

Compared to the Minoan and Mycenaean ages, Greek society in the Dark Age seemed to move backward. For example, the earlier civilizations each had their own form of writing. The Minoan alphabet is known as Linear A, and the Mycenaean alphabet, which was similar, is known as Linear B. After the Mycenaean civilization fell, Linear B was lost, and the people could no longer write.

This is why there are no written records of the Dark Age the way there are of the times before and after it. Everything historians know about this time in Greek history comes from **archaeological** finds.

The Minoans and Mycenaeans built huge, beautiful palaces. These were cultural centers where much of society's knowledge was kept. In the fall of Mycenaean society, the palaces were destroyed and abandoned. The same thing happened to the cities that had been built. People lived like they had before civilizations grew in Greece. They lived in small villages in places that were easy to guard from attackers. Because they were spread around like this instead of being one civilization, people's culture was a little bit different everywhere in Greece. A lot of it was still influenced by the Mycenaeans, though.

One way the Greeks advanced in the Dark Age was that they started using iron to make weapons and tools instead of bronze. Iron is better for these items because it is harder and sharper than bronze. However, archaeologists say the iron items they have found are not as well made as the earlier bronze ones. This shows that the Greeks also lost some of their metalworking skills.

## HOMER'S WRITING

Some of the most famous Greek writings are the *Iliad* and the *Odyssey*. Most people think they were both written by a man named Homer. He lived toward the end of the Dark Age and wrote down stories that had been passed down **orally** for hundreds of years. His writing reminded the Greeks that they shared a common history and culture, and they inspired other works of art that helped bring ancient Greece out of the Dark Age.

This statue of Homer sits outside the University of Athens. His writing was very important to the ancient Greeks.

The Greeks often built the center of their city-states on top of a hill. This was called the acropolis, or "high city." Many modern-day towns in Greece have the remains of an old acropolis.

# CHAPTER THREE

## GREEK CITY-STATES

Over time, the Greeks created more than 1,000 city-states. Some of the most important were Athens, Sparta, Corinth, Thebes, Syracuse, and Rhodes. Around 500 BCE, Athens started to grow into the largest of these. Athens was known for its art, **philosophy**, and poetry. Several great thinkers and poets lived and worked in Athens. The Parthenon, one of the greatest temples in Greece, was built at the top of the city.

### IMPORTANT IDEAS

Some of the things that were created in Athens are still used in countries around the world today. One of these is its court system. A group of people called a jury would hear both sides of an argument before deciding who was to blame. In other ancient civilizations, rulers often made these decisions, so this was a new idea.

Another thing many countries have today is a system of government called democracy. The word "democracy" comes from the Greek word *demos*, which means "citizens" or "the people." Greek city-states weren't ruled by a single person. In most city-states, all the male citizens were allowed to participate, or take part, in running the government. Women, enslaved people, and people who had moved to Greece from other countries weren't considered citizens in ancient Greece. Today, democracies generally let all citizens of their country vote, and more than half of all countries in the world are democratic.

## RELIGION IN ANCIENT GREECE

The Greeks believed in a pantheon, or a group of gods and goddesses. This belief was a way for the ancient Greeks to understand and explain the natural world around them. The Greeks went to temples to worship their gods.

The most important gods in ancient Greece were the Olympian gods. They were believed to live on Mount Olympus and were led by Zeus, the greatest of them all.

### SAME GOD, DIFFERENT NAME

Because the Greeks had colonies in Italy, where the Roman Empire started, the Romans honored the same gods and goddesses until the Christian religion, or belief system, took over. However, the names were different in the Roman language. Today, many planets are named after Roman gods. For example, Jupiter is the Roman name for Zeus. The Disney movie *Hercules* takes place in Greece, and most of the gods have their Greek names—except the main character! Hercules is the Roman form of Herakles.

Temples were the center of city life because religion was very important to the Greeks. They believed the gods controlled everything, and they wanted to honor them all the time. In fact, the first Olympic Games were a series of sporting events held in honor of Zeus. The first recorded games were held in 776 BCE, but many experts think they were already 500 years old by that

These columns are all that is left of a huge temple that was built in Athens to honor Zeus.

time. People from city-states across the Greek world took part in the Olympics. They were banned by the Romans around 393 CE and did not start up again until 1896.

## A LONG PERIOD OF WAR

Beginning in 490 BCE, the Persian Empire tried to take over Greece. In order to win, the Greeks often fought in a tight line called a phalanx in which they used their shields to protect each other. The Greeks won the Persian War in 479 BCE.

Athens and Sparta, the two most powerful city-states in Greece, fought together during the Persian War. However, after the Persian War, Athens became very powerful. War then broke out between Athens and Sparta. The Peloponnesian War started around 431 BCE and lasted almost 30 years. Sparta finally defeated Athens in 404 BCE.

This drawing shows an Athenian leader named Pericles giving a speech at the end of the first year of the Peloponnesian War.

Unlike Athens, Sparta had a very warlike culture. This picture shows a Spartan (*left*) fighting a Persian (*right*) in the style of Greek pottery.

# CHAPTER FOUR

## UNITING THE COUNTRY

After the Peloponnesian War ended, Sparta took over Athens and set up an **oligarchy**. This upset the Athenians because they no longer had a say in their government. It also made other city-states, such as Thebes, nervous that Sparta was going to become too powerful. Those who supported democracy fought the oligarchs, and the oligarchs gave up control less than a year later. However, Athens was never again as powerful as it had been.

### THE END OF CITY-STATES

Athens, Sparta, and the other city-states did not last much longer. Philip II was the king of Macedonia, a kingdom north of Greece. Today, Macedonia is part of Greece, but most historians agree that the ancient Greeks did not consider it a Greek city-state. In 338 BCE, Philip II **conquered** Greece and united, or brought together, almost all of the Greek city-states into one country. This country became part of the Macedonian Empire.

## THE EMPIRE GROWS

Philip II got married seven times and had many children. However, his most famous child by far was Alexander the Great. In 336 BCE, Philip II was murdered. Alexander took over the throne when he was only 20 years old. He spent years expanding his empire, which was rooted in Greek culture. By 323 BCE, he controlled Egypt, Persia, and India. Between the earlier Greek colonies and Alexander's empire, the ancient Greeks spread their culture to a large part of the world.

When Alexander the Great took over Persia, he started following some of their customs, or cultural behaviors. He also ordered some of his army officers to marry Persian princesses to make the ties between Persia and the Macedonian Empire stronger.

This ancient Roman art shows Alexander the Great taking over the Italian city of Pompeii.

These changes were very unpopular with the Macedonians. Alexander died in 323 BCE, when he was only 32 years old. Some historians think he got sick, but others think he was killed.

## A HISTORIC RACE

An ancient Greek story says that in 490 BCE, a soldier ran about 25 miles (40 km) from Marathon to Athens to tell the Athenians that Greece had beaten the Persians. The first marathon was held at the first modern Olympic Games in 1896, and it retraced the route of the soldier's run. At the 1908 Olympics in London, England, extra length was added so the runners would finish in front of the king and queen. This extra length was kept, which is why all marathons are 26.2 miles (42.1 km) today.

## A LASTING IMPACT

Many buildings from ancient Greece have survived to the present day. Many of these buildings are temples. Greek styles still influence artists and builders. Many famous artists, such as Michelangelo, copied the styles of ancient Greek statues. Greek art continued to spread the influence of Greek culture around Europe. Columns such as those found on the Parthenon in Athens can be seen in buildings such as the Lincoln Memorial in Washington, D.C. Other things we can thank the ancient Greeks for include alarm clocks, umbrellas, maps, and certain math concepts.

Theater was another important Greek invention. Other civilizations told stories, but they were almost always used as a way of explaining the world around them, such as why the sun rises or why the rivers flood. The ancient Greeks told

The Lincoln Memorial (*shown here*) was influenced by Greek buildings.

stories like those, too, but they also wrote made-up stories just for enjoyment like the kind we read and watch today. They were the first to act them out on stage. Without the ancient Greeks, we might not have plays or movies today!

Ancient Greece was a civilization that grew from small villages to successful city-states. It faced a Dark Age and grew even stronger after it. Today, many people around the world can trace their family history back to Greece. They are often proud of the many things the Greeks invented and spread around the world.

# HISTORY HAPPENED HERE

## THE PARTHENON

- The Parthenon was a temple that was built to honor Athena, who watched over Athens.
- Over the years, it has also been used as a Catholic church and a Muslim mosque.
- When it was built, the Parthenon was colorfully painted.

## DELPHI

- The high priestess of the sun god Apollo lived at Delphi and gave people advice about the future. She was called the Oracle at Delphi.
- Today, visitors to the town of Delphi can see the remains of the Temple of Apollo (*shown here*).
- Another old building at Delphi is the stadium where the Pythian Games were held. These honored Apollo instead of Zeus.

## MYCENAE

- The remains of the Mycenaean civilization can be seen today near the town of Mykines, Greece.
- Visitors can see where the Mycenaeans lived and where they were buried.
- The Lion Gate (*shown here*) is one of the most famous parts of Mycenae.

# EVENTS DURING ANCIENT GREECE

| | |
|---|---|
| CA. 3000–1600 BCE | The Minoans rule around the Mediterranean Sea. |
| CA. 1550–1200 BCE | The Mycenaeans control mainland Greece. |
| CA. 1200–800 BCE | Ancient Greece goes through the Dark Age. |
| 776 BCE | The first recorded Olympic Games are held. |
| CA. 500 BCE | Athens begins to grow into the largest Greek city-state. |
| 490–479 BCE | Greece is invaded twice by the Persians before defeating them in the Persian War. |
| 431–404 BCE | The Peloponnesian War is fought between Athens and Sparta. |
| 338 BCE | Philip II of Macedonia conquers Greece. |
| 336 BCE | Alexander the Great takes over after the death of Philip II. |

# GLOSSARY

**archaeological:** Having to do with a branch of science that deals with past human life through the study of material remains of people who lived long ago.

**conquer:** To take control of by force.

**culture:** The beliefs and ways of life of a group of people.

**expand:** To make larger.

**expert:** Someone who has a special skill or knowledge.

**influence:** To have an effect on.

**isolate:** To keep apart from others.

**oligarchy:** A form of government where only a small group of people have a say in which laws and policies are made.

**orally:** By word of mouth.

**philosophy:** The study of ideas about knowledge, truth, and the nature and meaning of life.

**resource:** Something that is valuable to humans and can be used to make or do other things.

# FIND OUT MORE

## BOOKS

Bell, Samantha. *Ancient Greece*. Lake Elmo, MN: Focus Readers, 2020.

Edwards, Roberta. *Where Is the Parthenon?* New York, NY: Grosset & Dunlap, 2016.

Scarborough, Kate. *Ancient Greece*. New York, NY: DK Publishing, 2020.

## WEBSITES

**BBC: Ancient Greece**
*www.bbc.co.uk/education/topics/z87tn39*
Learn more about what family life, mythology, war, and art were like in ancient Greece.

**British Museum: Ancient Greece**
*www.ancientgreece.co.uk/*
Pictures, stories, and activities make ancient Greece come alive.

**Ducksters: Ancient Greece for Kids**
*www.ducksters.com/history/ancient_greece.php*
This website contains articles covering many topics about ancient Greece, including its government, important people, and culture.

**Publisher's note to educators and parents:** Our editors have carefully reviewed these websites to ensure that they are suitable for students. Many websites change frequently, however, and we cannot guarantee that a site's future contents will continue to meet our high standards of quality and educational value. Be advised that students should be closely supervised whenever they access the internet.

# INDEX